Changing Schools

by Jane Manners
Illustrated by R. W. Alley

I really miss my old school.
It was as perfect as could be.

I never had to ride a bus…

or line up by a tree.

I never had to make new friends.

I never felt so sad.

But wait...

maybe Mom and Dad were right.
This new school is not so bad.